OWLS

Published by Creative Education, Inc., 123 South Broad Street, Mankato, Minnesota 56001

Printed by permission of Wildlife Education, Ltd.

ISBN 0-88682-268-8

OWLS

Created by
Quality Productions, Inc.

Written by
Timothy Levi Biel

Editorial Consultant
John Bonnett Wexo

Zoological Consultant
Charles R. Schroeder, D.V.M.
Director Emeritus
San Diego Zoo &
San Diego Wild Animal Park

Scientific Consultants
Arthur Crane Risser, Ph.D.
Curator of Birds
San Diego Zoo

Kenton C. Lint
Curator of Birds Emeritus
San Diego Zoo

Creative Education

Art Credits

Pages Eight and Nine: Trevor Boyer: **Pages Twelve and Thirteen: Main Art,** Trevor Boyer; **Pages Twelve and Thirteen: Sidebar,** Walter Stuart; **Pages Sixteen and Seventeen: Main Art,** Trevor Boyer; **Page Sixteen: Bottom Left,** Ed Zilberts; **Page Seventeen: Top,** Rebecca Bliss; **Page Eighteen:** Walter Stuart; **Page Nineteen: Top,** Walter Stuart; **Bottom,** Rebecca Bliss; **Pages Twenty and Twenty-one: Main Art,** Trevor Boyer; **Page Twenty: Bottom,** Raoul Espinoza; **Pages Twenty and Twenty-one: Top,** Rebecca Bliss; **Page Twenty-one: Bottom,** Walter Stuart.

Photographic Credits

Cover: Rod Williams *(Bruce Coleman, Inc.);* **Pages Six and Seven:** John Daniels *(Ardea London);* **Page Eight:** Doug Wilson *(West Stock);* **Page Nine: Top Left,** William Boehm *(West Stock);* **Top Right,** *(Grant Heilman);* **Bottom Right,** *(Grant Heilman);* **Page Ten: Top Right,** Pekka Helo *(Bruce Coleman Ltd.);* **Middle Left,** Liz & Tony Bomford *(Survival Anglia);* **Middle Right,** Leonard Lee Rue III *(Bruce Coleman Ltd.);* **Bottom Right,** C. B. & D. W. Frith *(Bruce Coleman Inc.);* **Page Eleven: Top Left,** Hans Reinhard *(Bruce Coleman Inc.);* **Top Middle,** Hans Reinhard *(Bruce Coleman Ltd.);* **Top Right,** Kenneth Fink *(Bruce Coleman Inc.)* **Bottom Right,** E. Breeze Jones *(Bruce Coleman Ltd.);* **Page Thirteen:** C. W. Schwartz *(Animals Animals);* **Pages Fourteen and Fifteen:** Hans Reinhard *(Bruce Coleman Inc.);* **Page Sixteen:** Richard Leonhardt; **Page Seventeen: Top Left,** C. F. E. Smedley *(Natural Science Photos);* **Top Right,** R. J. C. Blewitt *(Ardea London);* **Middle Left,** Dennis W. Schmidt *(Valan Photos);* **Middle Right,** Richard Leonhardt: **Bottom Left,** Hans Reinhard *(Bruce Coleman Inc.);* **Bottom Right,** Stefan Meyets *(Animals Animals);* **Page Eighteen: Middle,** George H. Harrison *(Grant Heilman);* **Bottom Left,** Michel Julien *(Valan Photos);* **Bottom Middle,** Steven Kaufman *(Peter Arnold Inc.);* **Bottom Right,** John Daniels *(Ardea London);* **Page Nineteen: Top,** Em Ahart; **Middle,** Phil Schofield *(West Stock);* **Bottom,** Jan Burton *(Bruce Coleman Ltd.);* **Page Twenty-one: Top Left,** C. Allan Morgan; **Top Right,** Alan D. Briere *(Tom Stack & Assoc.);* **Middle,** J. Senser *(Alpha/FPG);* **Bottom,** E. Breeze Jones *(Bruce Coleman Ltd.);* **Pages Twenty-two and Twenty-three;** Jeff Foote *(Bruce Coleman Inc.).*

Our Thanks To: Bernard Thornton; Derek Read *(British Museum, Tring);* Susan Breis, Sarah Feuerstein, Dr. Amadeo Rea *(San Diego Museum of Natural History);* Ed Hamilton *(San Diego Bionomics);* Pat Burke *(U.S. Soil Conservation Service);* Pam Stuart, Andy Lucas.

Creative Education would like to thank Wildlife Education, Ltd., for granting them the right to print and distribute this hardbound edition.

Contents

Owls _____ 6 - 7

Different kinds of owls _____ 8 - 9

Recognizing owls is easy _____ 10 - 11

An owl's body _____ 12 - 13

Hunting at night _____ 16 - 17

Owls play an important role _____ 18 - 19

A mother owl _____ 20 - 21

The future _____ 22 - 23

Index _____ 24

Owls are mysterious creatures. We often think of them as being scary, or even evil. They live in abandoned houses that may seem haunted. They fly through churchyards and cemeteries at night. In stories, they appear with witches, ghosts, and goblins. And when we hear an owl's familiar "who ... who," it sends shivers down our spines.

But why? Perhaps the owls' night habits make them seem spooky. They fly so quietly, it is as if they appear out of nowhere—like ghosts on wings. They fly and even hunt on the darkest of nights. Their eyes seem to glow in the dark. It makes us wonder what strange powers these birds possess.

Owls do possess *unusual* powers of sight and hearing, but they are completely natural. And really, there is *no* reason to fear owls. In fact, they are very helpful animals. By hunting mice and other rodents, they help to maintain a natural balance of plant and animal life. Without owls, rodents would overrun farmers' fields and storage barns.

As you will discover, there are many different kinds of owls in the world. In all, there are over 130 species, and they vary greatly in size. Eurasian Eagle Owls may measure nearly 5 feet (1.5 meters) from wingtip to wingtip. But the Least Pygmy Owl, with its one-foot (30-centimeter) wingspan, isn't much bigger than a robin.

Most male and female owls of the same species look alike, although the females are usually larger. And in some species, such as the Snowy Owl, the female's colors make her harder to see in the trees or grass where she makes her nest. This protects her from enemies while she sits on her eggs or cares for her young.

Baby owls are usually called *chicks*. The chicks stay with their mothers and fathers until they are about 3 months old. Then they find their own hunting territories, where they may stay for the rest of their lives. And they can live to be almost 20 years old.

In this book, you will learn many things about owls. But in some ways, they will always remain mysterious.

Different kinds of owls live all around the world. They are found on every continent except Antarctica. And they live in many different kinds of places.

Some owls can live in cold climates, and others in warm climates. They may live in dry deserts or rainy jungles. Many owls like wide open spaces, while others stay hidden in the forests.

There are owls living everywhere. So no matter where *you* live, you probably have several different kinds of owls living near you.

CHESTNUT-BACKED OWLET

TUNDRA

SNOWY OWL

This owl lives in the cold, northern *tundra*, where it blends in well with the surroundings. Its long, warm coat of feathers reaches right down to its toes. Even its bill is covered by snowy white feathers.

8

Tropical jungles are home to many small owls, like the one at left. Its small wingspan enables it to fly through the jungle without crashing into trees. And its beautiful red feathers are dark enough for hiding in the shadows.

LONG-EARED OWL

FOREST

Most owls live in heavily wooded areas. By day, they sleep in trees, where their colors make them hard to see. At night, many of them, like the Long-eared Owl at left, hunt for mice along the meadows and roadways near the edge of the forest.

BARN OWL

OPEN FIELDS

A white face shaped like a heart makes this owl easy to recognize. Barn Owls usually live near farms, all around the world. They hunt in open fields. And as you may have noticed, they have longer wings than most owls. These are best for flying over open country where there are few trees.

Recognizing owls is easy. Just look for a round face, big eyes, and a sharp, hooked bill. The face is almost completely covered by two large discs, called *facial discs* (FAY-shul disks). Many owls also have feathers sticking up on their heads that look like ears. These are called *ear tufts*.

It is *not* easy to tell one kind of owl from another. You have to look very carefully. For a few minutes, pretend you are a scientist studying birds. Look closely at the owls pictured on these pages, but don't read about them yet. Just see what differences you can pick out.

For example, do the facial discs of some owls look different than others? Do you see some owls *with* ear tufts, and others *without*? Do those with ear tufts all look the same? What other differences do you see? After you have studied these owls, read the captions and see how well you did.

Did you notice how big this owl's face is? It has the largest facial discs of any owl. And its unusually small eyes make these discs look even bigger.

GREAT GRAY OWL

EASTERN SCREECH OWL

PEL'S FISHING OWL

Did you notice anything different about the legs on this owl? They don't have feathers. Fishing Owls do not need feathers on their legs to protect them from their prey. Besides, these feathers would just get wet and cold.

Recognizing birds in the wild is tricky, because you don't always get a good look at them. If you saw this owl flying overhead, would you notice its gray color, or the stripes under its wings? Would you see the ear tufts, or the small, oval discs on its face? If so, you would probably know that this owl is an Eastern Screech Owl.

MALAYSIAN EAGLE OWL

Here's an Eagle Owl that's easy to recognize. It has extremely long ear tufts that stick straight out on the *sides* of its head.

These two have very striking faces. Their ear tufts and facial discs line up to make a "V" on their foreheads. Most Scops Owls have noticeable ear tufts and bushy feathers that cover their beaks like moustaches.

COLLARED SCOPS OWLS

From head to toe, this is a very typical owl. Like many owls, it has ear tufts sticking up on its head. And like most owls, its legs and feet have a thick covering of feathers. This protects them from snakes, rats, and other prey that bite.

Compare this owl's face with the others shown here. Do the other faces look rounder? They should, because Bay Owls and Barn Owls have faces that are shaped like a heart.

THAILAND BAY OWL

YOUNG TAWNY OWL AND ADULT

Young owls do not look like their parents. For example, *adult* Tawny Owls have reddish brown feathers, large heads, wide, round facial discs, and big black eyes. *Young* Tawny Owls have fluffy white feathers. And their eyes are dark blue. Can you tell the young Tawny Owl in this picture from its parent?

An owl's body is ideal for night living. Its superb senses help it to hunt in the dark. For example, owls have the best night vision of any creature on earth. And their hearing is almost as remarkable. An owl can hear the tiny sound of a mouse stepping on a twig from 75 feet away (23 meters).

Owls look the way they do because of these night senses. Their heads have to be large because they have huge eyes and ears. The skull is broad so that both eyes look forward, which makes the owl's vision more accurate. And believe it or not, their facial discs help owls hear better. In these and many other ways, the owl's body is built to make the best possible use of its senses.

Owls can hear better than other birds. One reason for this is the size of the *ear openings* in their skulls. Most birds just have little holes for ears, but owls have a gigantic hole on each side of the skull.

The position of its eyes helps an owl see better. You can't focus sharply on something unless you see it with both eyes at the same time. Most birds have eyes on the sides of their heads, and they only see a tiny area with both eyes. But the owl's eyes look straight ahead, so it sees more clearly. The orange areas in the pictures below show where most birds can focus Ⓐ, and where an owl can focus Ⓑ.

Ⓐ   Ⓑ

Most animals that are active at night have big eyes. This allows them to catch almost every bit of light available. But an owl's eyes are *so* big, they have no room to move up, down, or even sideways.

Imagine that your eyes cannot move, and you can only look straight ahead, like an owl. Your head will only turn far enough to the right and left to let you see what is *in front of you* ①.

Since its eyes cannot move, an owl must keep turning its head to follow a moving object. Luckily, its neck is so flexible that it seems to be made of rubber.

An owl can turn its neck so far, and so fast, it sometimes looks as though the head is just spinning like a top!

An owl can turn its head so far to the right ② that it sees what is behind it. In fact, it can keep turning until it is actually looking over its *left shoulder!* And it can turn its head so far to the left ③ that it ends up looking over the *right shoulder.*

Starting with its head already turned as far as it will go one way, an owl can then turn its head the other way a full circle and a half! ④

Ear tufts aren't ears at all. In fact, owls do not have noticeable ears like ours. They just have big holes hidden behind their facial discs. But these discs work something like our ears. They help funnel sound into the ear openings. An owl can even move its facial discs back and forth slightly, to pick up sounds from different angles.

The wings of most birds have stiff feathers that make noise when they fly Ⓐ. But the feathers on an owl's wing have soft edges Ⓑ, so it can fly more quietly. This way, the owl can listen carefully for its prey, and fly close to them without being heard.

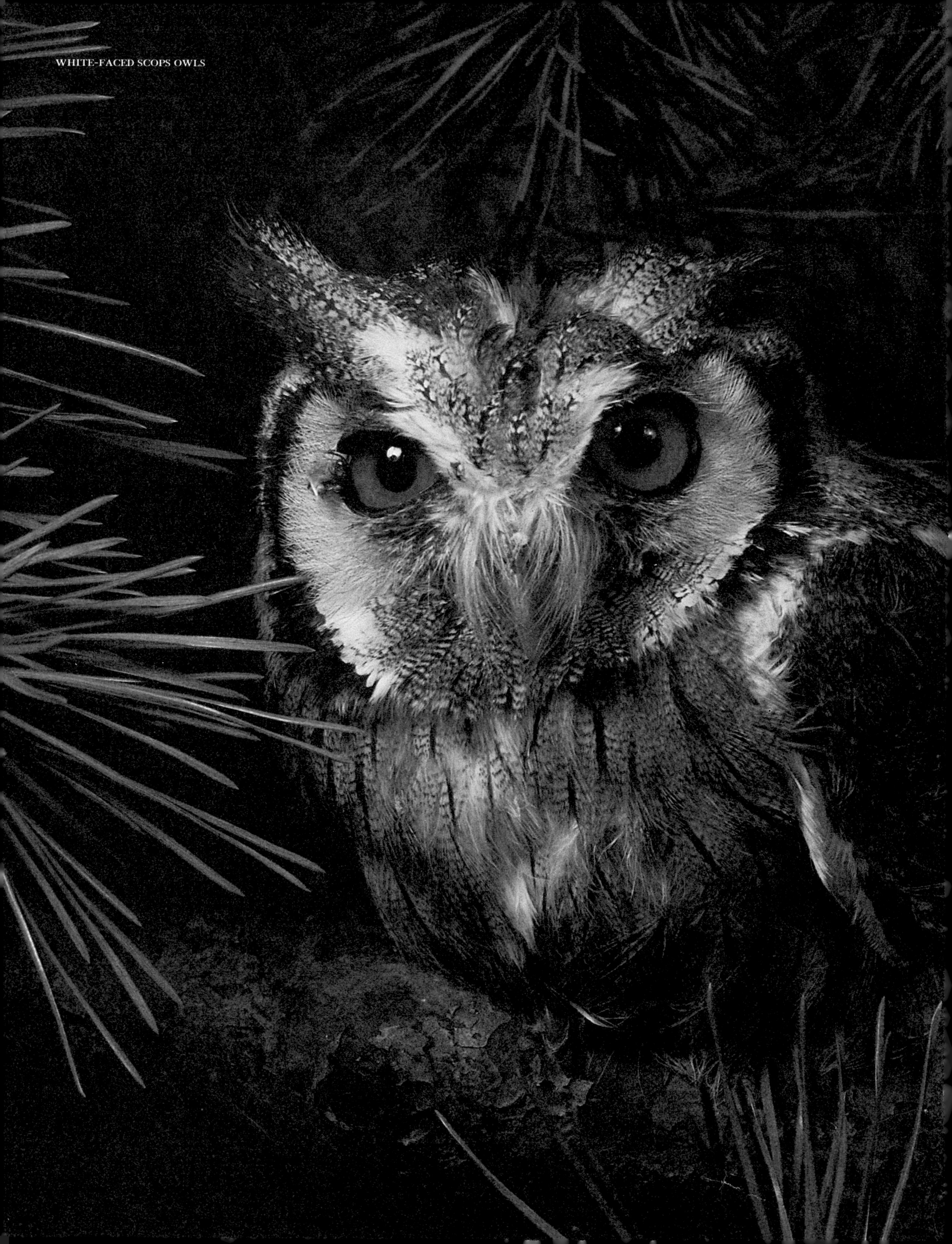

Hunting at night is something that owls do better than any other bird. When hawks and eagles sleep, the owls take over. They hunt in the same areas, and they hunt many of the same kinds of prey. But because of the darkness, owls must use different hunting skills.

When they hunt, owls do not soar like eagles. They do not use long range vision like hawks. Instead, they fly close to the ground, listening and watching for their prey in the dark.

To hunt, an owl perches silently on a branch. Then it watches and listens for any movement below ①.

An owl's *talons* (TAL-uns), or claws, are dangerous weapons. The way they stab and hold their prey works like the ice hook below, which stabs and holds slippery blocks of ice. Once an animal is in the owl's grasp, it rarely escapes.

When an owl attacks, it spreads all 8 of its toes as far as they'll stretch. This gives the owl a better chance of grabbing its prey in the dark.

SEE FOR YOURSELF why an owl spreads its talons so wide. Place a tiny wad of paper in front of you. Close your eyes and try to touch the paper, using only *one* finger. Now try spreading *all* your fingers as wide as you can. You have a much better chance of striking the paper this way. And that's the way it works for the owl, too.

When it sees or hears an animal below, the owl swoops down and flies close to the ground. As it comes closer and closer, it stops beating its wings and glides in for the attack ②.

After capturing its prey, the owl flies back to its perch ③. Unless it has something big, like a rabbit, it carries the prey in its bill ④.

②

⑤

④

Owls usually swallow their prey whole—even the teeth, bones, and fur. If the prey is too large, the owl breaks it into pieces. But it still swallows bones and all ⑤.

PELVIS AND
LEG BONES OF RAT

PELLET

SKULL AND TEETH OF RAT

The owl cannot digest everything that it swallows. Some things, like teeth, bones, and hair, are packed into *pellets* and spit out. If you find owl pellets and gently take them apart, you can see what an owl has eaten.

The sharp beak is used to tear pieces of meat that are too large to swallow whole. Although it looks dangerous, the bill is never used as a weapon. Owls always use their claws for that.

QUAIL

Ⓐ

UPSIDE-DOWN CATFISH

Ⓑ

ROE DEER

Ⓒ

Owls can capture a wide variety of prey. Many catch birds Ⓐ. Fishing owls eat mostly fish Ⓑ. And Eagle Owls sometimes even take young deer Ⓒ.

Owls play an important role in nature.

Whether we realize it or not, owls affect our lives every day. They help us by controlling rodents and insects.

We tend to forget this, though. And we sometimes even treat owls as our enemies. But they are really the enemies of insects, rodents, and small birds. If it weren't for owls and other predators, the numbers of these animals would zoom out of control.

As it is, owls and their prey are locked in a constant fight for survival. Of course, owls must also compete with each other. And this usually makes them bitter rivals. But as you see in the box at the bottom of the page, some owls solve the problem of competition in a more peaceful way.

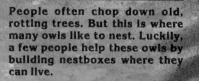

People often chop down old, rotting trees. But this is where many owls like to nest. Luckily, a few people help these owls by building nestboxes where they can live.

Every owl has its own *territory*, or hunting area. It usually patrols its "borders" to keep other owls out. However, owls of *different species* sometimes share the same territory. They get along by hunting at different times of day, or for different kinds of prey. For example, a Great Gray Owl, a Ural Owl, and a Tawny Owl may all three share the same territory. The Great Gray Owl is a daytime hunter. Despite its large size, it hunts almost entirely for little rodents called *voles*.

GREAT GRAY OWL

URAL OWL

The Ural Owl can hunt by day or night. But instead of hunting for voles, it usually looks for larger prey, like squirrels.

You may also find a Tawny Owl patrolling the same territory. It hunts voles, but avoids the Great Gray Owl by hunting only at night.

TAWNY OWL

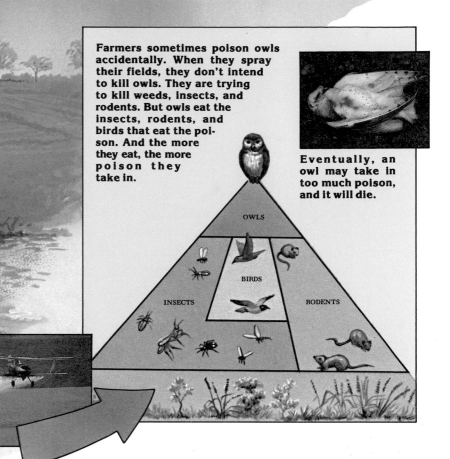

Farmers sometimes poison owls accidentally. When they spray their fields, they don't intend to kill owls. They are trying to kill weeds, insects, and rodents. But owls eat the insects, rodents, and birds that eat the poison. And the more they eat, the more poison they take in.

Eventually, an owl may take in too much poison, and it will die.

OWLS

BIRDS

INSECTS

RODENTS

Owls help farmers by keeping rodents and small birds away. Unfortunately, a few farmers are not always helpful to owls. As you see at right, their methods of controlling pests can be harmful.

LONG-EARED OWL

Owls can be very unfriendly to other animals. They don't even like other owls. If they see one, they usually spread their wings, fluff up their feathers, and hiss loudly. This is called a *threat display*, and it is meant to scare the intruder away.

Owls are the deadly enemies of small birds. Sometimes mobs of these little birds will all fly toward an owl at once. Usually the owl is startled, but not hurt. The small birds are just delivering a message: "We know you're there, so don't try sneaking up on us!"

19

A mother owl gives her little chicks constant care for almost 3 months. She feeds them, protects them from danger, and teaches them to fly and hunt. By the time the chicks are 3 months old, they must be expert hunters. That is when they leave their parents and find territories of their own.

The father owl often helps the mother raise their young. They may find a nest together, and the father may even take his turn sitting on the eggs. After they hatch, he goes hunting and brings back food for the whole family.

Considering how independent adult owls are, it is amazing to see how well mother and father owls can cooperate. But first, they must overcome their natural fear of each other. And this begins as soon as the male courts the female, as you see at right.

When he thinks a female is watching him, he lands and drops his prey. With his wings and tail outspread, he struts around the lemming ②.

In the spring, male owls behave in special ways to attract females. For example, the male Snowy Owl carries a lemming in its beak and flies around beating its wings wildly up and down ①.

It takes most young owls about 6 months before they look like adults. But Spectacled Owls, like those shown below, keep their beautiful white body feathers and dark faces for about 5 years.

The younger brothers and sisters in this family of Spectacled Owls are too young to fly. As with most owl families, there is an age difference of about two days between each of the chicks. Can you tell which of them is the youngest of all?

The number of eggs an owl lays depends on its supply of food. In years when prey is scarce, the owl may lay no eggs at all Ⓐ. If the number of prey is small, it may lay 2 or 3 eggs Ⓑ. And in years with plenty of food, there will also be plenty of eggs Ⓒ.

If a female approaches him, he turns his back to her and hides the lemming with his wing. He continues to do this while she gradually moves closer. This may go on for hours, but slowly, they begin to lose their fear of each other ③.

Most owls live in trees, but some live in rather unusual places. The family of Screech Owls (above) has moved into an abandoned woodpecker hole in a giant cactus. Barn Owls (top right) often make their homes in the rafters of barns or vacant buildings. And the Burrowing Owl (below right) lives in underground burrows.

This mother Owl is teaching her month-old chicks to fly. With each flight, she increases the distance slightly. And flapping their wings wildly, the chicks try to follow her.

Owls have no fear when it comes to protecting their young. They will swoop down on anything—or anyone—that disturbs their nest. And they strike wildly at the invader with their sharp claws.

Chicks usually hatch two days apart. The oldest chicks grow up to be the strongest, because they get most of the food. When food is scarce, only the oldest chicks get enough to survive. This may seem harsh, but it is nature's way of making sure that at least *some* owls will live.

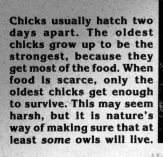

21

The future of most owls looks promising—if we are willing to help. People can help owls survive in several ways. The first thing we can do is stop people from poisoning them. We must teach others that poisons are not the *only* way to control rodents and other pests. Unless they are used with extreme caution, these poisons can kill owls, other predators, and maybe even humans.

On the other hand, owls and other predators can help us control pests, if we let them. But they need trees to live in, and land where they can hunt. It is important to leave them enough natural land so they can make their homes and hunt their prey.

That's easier to do for some owls than it is for others. In this century, many of the world's forests have been cleared to make room for cities and farms. This isn't a problem for Barn Owls, Little Owls, Short-eared Owls, and others that like open spaces. Even many woodland owls, such as the Tawny Owl, the Screech Owl, and the Long-eared Owl, have adjusted well to changes in their habitat.

But other owls have not been so lucky. For example, the Spotted Owl lives in dense evergreen forests and wooded canyons in the western United States. In recent years, people have cleared entire forests to provide lumber for homes and other buildings. This has threatened the survival of the Spotted Owl.

The world's largest owls, the Eurasian Eagle Owls, are also in danger. These owls need large hunting territories and large prey, such as rabbits, ducks, and snakes. But they live in heavily populated areas of the world, where these animals are not easy to find.

We can help these and other owls by setting aside wilderness areas where they can live. We can enforce laws that protect owls from being hunted and senselessly killed. And if we must cut down trees, we can put up nextboxes that will make it easier for some owls to live near cities and towns. Working together, we can build a promising future for owls throughout the world.

If you would like to learn how to build a nestbox, write to the following address and ask for "Barn Owl Nestbox Plans":

Soil Conservation Service
1523 E. Valley Parkway, #205
Escondido, California 92027

Index

Attack behavior, 16
Baby owls, 6
See also Chicks.
Barn owls, 9, 22
    Chicks of, 21
Beak, 17
Body, 12-13
Burrowing owls, 21
Camouflage, 6
    Of Snowy owls, 8
Chestnut-backed owlet, 8
Chicks, 6
    Flying lessons for, 21
    Protection of, 20, 21
    Survival of oldest, 21
Claws, 16
Collared Scops owls, 11
Coloring
    Of Eastern Screech owl, 10
    As protection, 6
Courting behavior, 20-21
Differences among owls, 10
Digestion, 17
Ear openings, 12
Ear tufts, 10, 13
Eastern Screech owl, 10
Eggs
    Numbers laid, 20
Endangered owls, 22
Eurasian Eagle owls, 6, 11, 22
Eyes
    Position of, 12
    Size of, 12, 13
Face shape
    Of Barn owls, 9
Facial discs, 10
    As a help to hearing, 12, 13
    Of the Great Gray owl, 10
Farmers
    Owls as helpers to, 19
Father owls, 20
Fear of owls, 6
Feathers
    On the head, 10
    On the wings, 13

Female owls, 6
See also Mother owls.
Flying
    While hunting, 16
    At night, 6
Food
    Birds and fish as, 17
    Swallowing food whole, 17
Forests
    As owls' home, 9
Future of owls, 22
Great Gray owl, 10
    As a daytime hunter, 18
Habitats, 8
    Adjustment to changes in, 22
Head
    Ability to turn, 13
Hearing, 12
Hunting, 6
See also Night hunting.
    Steps in, 16-17
Kinds of owls, 6, 8-9
Least Pygmy owl, 6
Legs
    Lack of feathers on, 10
Life span, 6
Little owls, 22
Living quarters, 21
Long-eared owls, 9, 22
Malaysian Eagle owl, 10
Male owls, 6
Mice
    Hunting of, 6, 9
Mother owls, 20
Nature
    Owls' role in, 18
Neck
    Flexibility of, 13
Nestboxes
    Building, 18, 22
Nesting
    Areas for, 18
Night habits, 6
Night hunting, 16-17
Night senses, 12

Night vision, 12
Owl pellets, 17
Owl prey, 17
Owls
    As mysterious creatures, 6
    Recognizing, 10
    As rivals, 18
    Unfriendliness of, 19
    Ways humans can help, 22
Pel's Fishing owl, 10
Pests
    Owl control of, 22
Poisoning of owls, 19, 22
Rodents
    Control of, 18
    Hunting of, 6
Screech owls, 21, 22
Senses
    Development of, 12
Short-eared owls, 22
Small birds
    As owl prey, 19
Snowy owls, 6, 8
Soil Conservation Service, 22
Species of owls, 6
Spectacled owls, 20
Spotted owls, 22
Squirrels
    As owl prey, 18
Talons, 16
Tawny owls, 11, 18, 22
Territory, 18
Thailand Bay owl, 11
Threat display, 19
Tropical jungles
    As owls' home, 9
Tundra, 8
Ural owls, 18
White-faced Scops owl, 14-15
Wilderness, preserving, 22
Wing feathers, 13
Wing span, 6
    Of Barn owls, 9
    Of jungle owls, 9